Exploring China 2023

A Comprehensive Travel Handbook To Zhangye Danxia Geopark, China

Fodor Elise

Table Of Contents

Chapter One

Welcome To China

China, officially the People's Republic of China (PRC), is a country in East Asia. It is the world's most populous country, with a population of over 1.4 billion. Beijing is the capital of China and its largest city.

China is a socialist state governed by the Communist Party of China, with President Xi Jinping as its General Secretary. The country covers an area of approximately 9.6 million square kilometers and is the third largest country in the world. China has a long and rich history, with a civilization dating back to ancient times.

It is also known for its contributions to art, literature, and science. In recent years, China has become a major economic and military power, and it plays a central role in international affairs.

China has a diverse culture and geography, with many ethnic groups and regions. The main language spoken is Mandarin Chinese, but there are also many other languages and dialects spoken throughout the country. The Chinese economy is the second largest in the world and has been growing rapidly in recent years.

The country has become a major exporter of goods, and its manufacturing industry is one of the largest in the world.

China is also a major player in the global technology industry, and it is home to many major tech companies such as Huawei, Tencent, and Alibaba.

China has a complex relationship with the international community. While it is a member of the United Nations and the World Trade Organization, it has been criticized by many countries for its human rights record and territorial disputes with its neighbors.

China's relations with the United States have been particularly tense in recent years, due to issues such as trade, human rights, and territorial disputes in the South China Sea.

In terms of tourism, China offers a wide variety of attractions, including historical sites such as the Great Wall of China and the Terracotta Army, as well as natural wonders such as the Yangtze River and the Yellow Mountains. It is also known for its delicious cuisine and its traditional arts, such as calligraphy and martial arts.

China also has a rapidly developing infrastructure, with major investments in transportation, such as high-speed trains and modern airports. The country is home to many of the world's tallest and largest buildings, including the Shanghai Tower and the Hong Kong-Zhuhai-Macau Bridge.

In recent years, China has also been working to promote its soft power, by investing in cultural and education exchanges, and promoting the study of the Chinese language and culture abroad.

China is also a major player in global politics, being a permanent member of the United Nations Security Council and playing an active role in international organizations such as the G20 and the World Health Organization. The country is also a major contributor to peacekeeping operations and humanitarian aid around the world.

China's economy also continues to grow and evolve, with an increasing focus on innovation, technology and services sectors, as well as "green" and sustainable development. Additionally, the country is also promoting its own "belt and road" initiative, a large-scale infrastructure and investment project, to connect Asia, Europe, and Africa.

Overall, China is a country with a complex and dynamic society and economy, with a rapidly developing infrastructure and an increasing global influence. The country continues to evolve and change, making it an important and interesting country to study and understand.

Chapter Two

Zhangye Danxia Geopark, China

The Zhangye Danxia Geopark is a UNESCO World Heritage Site located in Gansu Province, China. It is known for its colorful rock formations that have been formed by red sandstone and mineral deposits.

The park covers an area of 510 square kilometers and features unique landscapes, including peaks, pillars, towers, and ravines. Visitors can hike through the park to see the various rock formations and take in the beautiful scenery. The park is also home to several temples and monasteries, as well as a number of rare and endangered species of plants and animals.

The Zhangye Danxia Geopark is also known for its colorful sunrise and sunset views, which are a popular attraction for visitors. The park has several scenic spots, such as Rainbow Mountains, The First Bend of the Yellow River, and The Temple of the Bearded Dragon, among others. The Rainbow Mountains, in particular, are a must-see for visitors, as the multi-colored layers of rock create a stunning display of colors that change throughout the day.

The park is also home to several cultural and historical sites, including the Temple of the Bearded Dragon, which is a Buddhist temple dating back to the Tang Dynasty.
The temple is known for its intricate carvings and sculptures, as well as its beautiful gardens.

To fully experience the park, it is recommended to stay overnight in one of the nearby towns and take a guided tour to explore the different scenic spots and historical sites.

The park is also a great spot for adventure activities like rock climbing, paragliding, and hot-air balloon rides. With the beautiful landscapes, cultural and historical sites, and adventure activities, the Zhangye Danxia Geopark is a must-visit destination for any traveler in China.

Chapter Three

My Experience In Zhangye Danxia Geopark, China

The first experience in Zhangye Danxia Geopark was one that I will never forget. I had always been fascinated by the country and its culture, and I was thrilled when I finally had the opportunity to visit.

As I approached Zhangye Danxia Geopark, I couldn't help but feel a sense of excitement and awe. The park's unique and colorful rock formations were unlike anything I had ever seen before.

The vibrant hues of red, orange, yellow, and green seemed to glow in the sunlight, creating a truly breathtaking sight.

As I entered the park, I immediately made my way to the highest peak, Danxia Peak. The hike to the top was challenging, but the stunning views from the summit made it well worth the effort. From the top, I could see the entire park spread out before me, the rainbow-colored rock formations stretching as far as the eye could see.

Next, I explored the many valleys and canyons that make up the park. Each one was more unique and beautiful than the last, with towering rock walls and winding streams.

I also came across some Buddhist temples and ancient Chinese architecture that were nestled among the rocks, adding an extra layer of history and culture to the experience.

Overall, my experience at Zhangye Danxia Geopark was truly unforgettable. The park's natural beauty and unique geology left me in awe and I would definitely recommend it to anyone visiting China.

As I continued my exploration of the park, I was struck by the diversity of the rock formations. Some were tall and pointed, while others were smooth and rounded.

I saw formations that resembled castles and towers, and others that looked like they had been shaped by water and wind over millions of years.

One of the highlights of my visit was the visit to the "Wave-Shaped Cliffs", where the red sandstone had been carved by erosion into undulating waves that seemed to go on forever. The vibrant colors and the unique shapes of the cliffs made for some truly mesmerizing views.

Another highlight of the trip was the visit to the "Five-Color Pond", which is a small lake located at the base of one of the rock formations. The lake is known for its striking colors, which change depending on the time of day and the weather.

It was truly a sight to behold, and I couldn't help but spend several minutes just taking in the beauty of the place.

As the day came to an end, I was sad to leave the park. The natural beauty, the unique geology and the history and culture that the park has to offer made for an unforgettable experience.

I would recommend Zhangye Danxia Geopark to anyone looking for a unique and beautiful destination in China. It is a place that will stay with me forever.

Chapter Four

Geography And Climate In China

China, the fourth largest country in the world, is located in East Asia and is bordered by 14 countries. Its terrain is varied and includes mountains, plateaus, and plains.

The Himalayas form the southern border of China, and the highest peak in China, Mount Everest, is located on the border of China and Nepal. The Tibetan Plateau, also known as the "Roof of the World," is located in the western part of the country and has an average elevation of 4,500 meters (14,764 ft).

The Gobi Desert and the Taklamakan Desert are located in the northern and northwestern regions of China, respectively. The Yangtze River, the longest river in China and the third longest in the world, runs through the country and is a major source of water, transportation, and hydroelectric power. The Yellow River, also known as the "Mother River of China," is located in the northern part of the country and is an important source of irrigation for agriculture.

China's climate is diverse, with the northern and northwestern regions experiencing a dry, continental climate, while the southern and southeastern regions have a humid, subtropical climate.

The northeastern region has a cold, continental climate, and the southwestern region has a temperate, monsoonal climate. The northern and northwestern regions of China experience a dry, continental climate, characterized by cold winters and hot summers.

The average temperature in January is around -15°C (5°F) and in July it is around 25°C (77°F). In the northeastern region, the climate is cold, continental, and characterized by long, cold winters and short, warm summers. The average temperature in January is around -20°C (-4°F) and in July it is around 20°C (68°F).

The southern and southeastern regions of China have a humid, subtropical climate, characterized by hot, humid summers and mild winters. The average temperature in January is around 10°C (50°F) and in July it is around 28°C (82°F). The southwestern region has a temperate, monsoonal climate, characterized by mild winters and hot summers. The average temperature in January is around 5°C (41°F) and in July it is around 25°C (77°F).

China is also susceptible to natural disasters such as floods, droughts, typhoons, and earthquakes. The Yangtze River and the Yellow River are known for causing devastating floods, and the northern and northwestern regions are prone to droughts.

The southeastern coast of China is frequently hit by typhoons, and the western part of the country is prone to earthquakes. In addition to the physical geography and climate of China, the country's geography also plays a significant role in its economic development.

The Yangtze River and the Yellow River are both major transportation routes for goods and resources, and the fertile soil along these rivers has led to the development of agriculture in these regions. The coastal regions of China, particularly those in the southeast, have also been important for economic development, as they have access to the sea for trade and fishing.

The mountainous regions of China, including the Himalayas and the Tibetan Plateau, have traditionally been less developed economically, but they are now becoming increasingly important for tourism and as sources of minerals and other resources. The Gobi Desert and the Taklamakan Desert have also been important for the development of natural resources, including oil and natural gas.

China's climate also plays an important role in its economy, particularly in the agricultural sector. The northern and northwestern regions of the country have a dry, continental climate, which is well-suited for growing crops such as wheat, corn, and barley.

The southern and southeastern regions have a humid, subtropical climate, which is ideal for growing crops such as rice, sugarcane, and fruits. The southwestern region has a temperate, monsoonal climate, which is well-suited for growing crops such as tea and tobacco.

China's geography and climate also have a significant impact on its culture and way of life. For example, the mountainous regions of China, such as Tibet and the Himalayas, have unique and distinct cultures that have developed over time due to their isolated location and challenging living conditions. Similarly, the dry, continental climate of the northern and northwestern regions has led to the development of nomadic cultures in these regions.

China's geography and climate have a significant impact on its economy, culture, and way of life. The diverse geography of the country, including its mountains, plateaus, plains, rivers, and deserts, has led to the development of different economic activities and cultures in different regions.

The climate also plays a major role in shaping the country's economy, particularly in the agricultural sector, and in the way of life of people. China's vulnerability to natural disasters such as floods, droughts, typhoons, and earthquakes is also a significant concern for the people and the government.

Chapter Five

History And Culture You Will Find China

China has a rich history and culture dating back thousands of years. The country has been shaped by a variety of dynasties, each leaving their mark on art, architecture, literature, philosophy, and more. Some of the most famous historical landmarks and cultural sites in China include the Great Wall, the Terracotta Army, the Forbidden City, and the Summer Palace.

Chinese culture is also known for its traditional art forms, such as calligraphy, painting, and martial arts, as well as its contributions to cuisine, such as Peking duck and Kung Pao chicken. Additionally, Confucianism, Taoism, and Buddhism have been three of the most influential philosophical and religious traditions in Chinese history.

Additionally, China has a long and rich tradition in literature, with famous works such as "Dream of the Red Chamber," "Journey to the West," and "Outlaws of the Marsh." The country is also known for its traditional festivals and celebrations, such as the Chinese New Year, the Mid-Autumn Festival, and the Dragon Boat Festival.

China has also played a major role in the development of science and technology. In ancient times, Chinese inventors and scientists made important contributions in fields such as astronomy, medicine, and engineering. For example, the ancient Chinese developed paper, gunpowder, the compass and printing.

Chinese culture is also deeply rooted in its traditional philosophy, which emphasizes the importance of harmony and balance in all aspects of life. This philosophy is reflected in many aspects of Chinese culture, such as the traditional martial art of Tai Chi and the practice of Feng Shui.

Finally, China is also known for its traditional performing arts, such as Peking Opera, Chinese acrobatics, and traditional dance. All these elements and many more make China a fascinating country with a rich cultural heritage.

Chapter Six

The Great Wall Of China

The Great Wall of China is a series of fortifications made of stone, brick, tamped earth, wood, and other materials, generally built along an east-to-west line across the historical northern borders of China to protect the Chinese states and empires against the raids and invasions of the various nomadic groups of the Eurasian Steppe.

Construction began in the 7th century BC and continued through the Ming dynasty (1368–1644). The Great Wall is the longest wall in the world, stretching over 13,000 miles.

It is also one of the most famous landmarks in the world and a popular tourist destination.

The Great Wall is not a single continuous wall, but is made up of many walls and fortifications built by different Chinese dynasties over the centuries. Some sections are wide enough for vehicles to drive on, while other sections are so narrow that only one person can walk through at a time.

The Great Wall was built using a variety of materials and techniques. The earlier sections, built during the 7th century BC, were made of rammed earth, while later sections were made of brick or stone.

The brick sections were often reinforced with tamped earth and stone. In some areas, the wall was also lined with stone or bricks.

The Great Wall was not only used for military defense, but also served as a border control mechanism, a transportation corridor, and a communication line. Watch towers, barracks and beacon towers were built along the wall for the soldiers to live and work. Additionally, the wall was a significant source of labor and resources for the Chinese Empire during its construction and maintenance.

Chapter Seven

The Terracotta Army

The Terracotta Army is a collection of terracotta sculptures depicting the armies of Qin Shi Huang, the first Emperor of China. The figures, dating from 210 BC, were discovered in 1974 by local farmers in the Lintong District, Xi'an, Shaanxi province, near the Mausoleum of the First Qin Emperor.

The Terracotta Army is a form of funerary art buried with the emperor in 210–209 BCE and whose purpose was to protect the emperor in his afterlife. The figures vary in height, uniform, and hairstyle in accordance with rank.

Most of the figures were originally painted, but due to the weathering and looting of the tombs, very little pigment remains. The figures are life-sized and are believed to have been created using molds.

The Terracotta Army is considered one of the greatest archaeological discoveries of the 20th century and is a UNESCO World Heritage Site. It is estimated that there are over 8,000 soldiers, 130 chariots with 520 horses and 150 cavalry horses, the majority of which are still buried in the pits near the emperor's mausoleum. The figures are arranged in battle formations, with the majority of them being infantry and the rest being archers, cavalry, and charioteers.

The figures are incredibly detailed, with unique facial expressions and detailed armor and clothing.

The discovery of the Terracotta Army has provided significant insight into the organization and technology of the ancient Chinese army.

The construction of the army is also considered a remarkable achievement in ancient Chinese engineering. The site has become a major tourist attraction and continues to be an important source of information for historians and archaeologists studying ancient Chinese history and culture.

In short, The Terracotta Army is a collection of thousands of life-sized terracotta sculptures depicting the armies of the first emperor of China, buried in 210-209 BCE to protect him in his afterlife. It's considered one of the greatest archaeological discoveries of the 20th century and a UNESCO World Heritage Site and tourist attraction.

Chapter Eight

The Forbidden Kingdom

The Forbidden Kingdom, also known as the Forbidden City, is a UNESCO World Heritage Site located in the heart of Beijing, China. It served as the imperial palace for the Ming and Qing dynasties from the 14th to the 20th century and was home to the emperor and his court.

The palace is surrounded by a moat and a high wall, which gave it its name, as it was off-limits to commoners for centuries. Today, it is open to the public and is one of the most popular tourist attractions in China.

The History of the Forbidden City

The Forbidden City, also known as the Palace Museum, was the Chinese imperial palace from the Ming dynasty to the end of the Qing dynasty in 1912. It is located in the center of Beijing, China and was built in the 15th century during the reign of the third Ming emperor, Yongle.

The palace complex was constructed over a 14-year period and served as the home of 24 emperors and their households. The palace was known as the “Forbidden City” because it was forbidden to enter without the emperor’s permission. The palace was declared a World Heritage Site in 1987 and is now open to the public as a museum.

The Forbidden City is a vast palace complex that covers over 720,000 square meters and contains over 9,000 rooms. The palace is divided into two main sections: the Outer Court, which was used for ceremonies and official business, and the Inner Court, which was the residence of the emperor and his family.

The palace also contains many important halls and structures, such as the Hall of Supreme Harmony, the Hall of Central Harmony, and the Hall of Preserving Harmony, which were used for important state ceremonies and events.

The palace is also known for its beautiful gardens and courtyards, which were designed to provide a peaceful retreat for the emperor and his family.

These gardens feature lakes, rockeries, and many other landscaping elements that were designed to create a harmonious and serene environment.

The Forbidden City was also home to many valuable works of art and cultural treasures. The palace's collection includes ceramics, jade, bronze, and other precious objects that were created by the finest artisans of the time. Some of these treasures are still on display at the Palace Museum today.

The palace was also the site of much political and historical significance. The Forbidden City was the center of imperial power for over 500 years, and many important events in Chinese history took place within its walls. The palace was seized by the Chinese republican revolutionaries in 1911, bringing an end to the imperial era. The palace was opened to the public in 1925 as the Palace Museum and has been open to visitors ever since.

The Architecture of the Forbidden City

The Forbidden City in Beijing, China, is a palace complex that was the home of the emperors of the Ming and Qing dynasties. The palace covers an area of 72 hectares (180 acres) and contains more than 9,000 rooms. The architecture of the Forbidden City is characterized by a combination of traditional Chinese and Mongolian styles, with influences from ancient palace architecture. The palace is divided into : the Outer Court, which was used for ceremonial purposes, and the Inner Court, which was the residence of the emperor and his family.

The palace is surrounded by a moat and a high wall, with four gates leading into the palace: the Meridian Gate, the Gate of Supreme Harmony, the Gate of Middle Harmony, and the Gate of Preserving Harmony. The palace also contains numerous halls, pavilions, courtyards, and gardens, as well as the Imperial Garden, which is a beautiful garden located in the northeastern corner of the palace.

The Forbidden City is a masterpiece of ancient Chinese architecture, with intricate details and symbolism woven into its design. The palace is laid out on a north-south axis, with the main entrance, the Meridian Gate, located at the southern end. The palace is divided into three main sections: the Outer Court, the Middle Court, and the Inner Court.

The Outer Court, also known as the Front Court, was used for ceremonial purposes and contains the Hall of Supreme Harmony, the Hall of Middle Harmony, and the Hall of Preserving Harmony. These halls were used for important state ceremonies, such as the emperor's enthronement and the reception of foreign envoys.

The Middle Court, also known as the Central Court, was the residence of the emperor and his family. It contains the Palace of Heavenly Purity, the Hall of Union, and the Palace of Earthly Tranquility. These halls were used for the emperor's daily life and also served as the living quarters for the emperor's consorts and children.

The Inner Court, also known as the Rear Court, was the residence of the empress and the imperial concubines. It contains the Palace of Tranquil Longevity, the Hall of Mental Cultivation, and the Imperial Garden.

The palace is surrounded by a moat and a high wall, with four gates leading into the palace: the Meridian Gate, the Gate of Supreme Harmony, the Gate of Middle Harmony, and the Gate of Preserving Harmony. Each gate has a unique design and significance, with the Meridian Gate considered the most important as it was the main entrance to the palace.

In addition to the palace buildings, the Forbidden City also contains numerous gardens, courtyards, and other features, such as the Imperial Garden and the Hall of Literary Glory. The palace is also adorned with many decorative elements, such as colorful glazed tiles, intricate carvings, and gold-leafed roofs.

The architectural design and decoration of the palace are rich in symbolism and reflect the political and cultural beliefs of the time.

The Treasures of the Forbidden City

The Treasures of the Forbidden City refers to the vast collection of art and artifacts housed within the Forbidden City, the imperial palace of the Chinese emperors in Beijing. The palace complex, which was built in the 15th century, contains over 9,000 rooms and is home to numerous rare and valuable objects, including ceramics, jade, bronze, and gold.

The collection also includes calligraphy, painting, and sculpture, as well as furniture, textiles, and other decorative arts.

Many of the items on display were commissioned for the palace or gifted to the emperor and are considered to be masterpieces of Chinese art and culture.

In addition to the art and artifacts, the Forbidden City also contains many architectural treasures, such as the Hall of Supreme Harmony, the Hall of Central Harmony, and the Hall of Preserving Harmony. These halls are considered some of the best examples of traditional Chinese palace architecture and are known for their intricate carvings, gold-gilded details, and colorful decorations.

The Forbidden City also houses several museums, such as the Palace Museum and the National Museum of China, which showcase some of the most valuable and significant items from the imperial collection. These museums are open to the public and are major tourist attractions in Beijing.

It is worth mentioning that the palace complex was closed to the public for almost 500 years, during the Ming and Qing dynasties, as it served as the residence of the emperor and his household, and was also where the emperor governed the country. After the fall of the Qing dynasty, it was opened to the public as a museum to showcase the art, culture and history of China.

The Life of the Imperial Court

Life at the Forbidden City was strictly regulated by a complex set of rules and rituals. The emperor and his court lived in a world of luxury and grandeur, but they were also isolated from the outside world.

The emperor was surrounded by a large number of eunuchs and courtiers, who were responsible for his every need. The imperial women, including the empress and the concubines, lived in a separate part of the palace and were not allowed to participate in politics.

The Forbidden City is a window into China's imperial past and offers a glimpse of the grandeur and opulence of the imperial court. Its architecture, treasures, and history make it a must-see destination for anyone interested in Chinese culture and history.

Visiting the Forbidden City is a unique and unforgettable experience, and it is easy to understand why it has remained one of China's most popular tourist attractions for centuries.

Chapter Nine

The Summer Palace

The Summer Palace in Beijing, China is a large imperial garden and palace complex that was used by the emperors of the Qing Dynasty as a place of rest and recreation. The palace is located in the western suburbs of Beijing and covers an area of over 3 square kilometers.

The Summer Palace was first built in 1750 during the reign of Emperor Qianlong, and was originally named "Qingyi Garden" (Garden of Clear Ripples). It was later renamed "Yiheyuan" (Garden of Health and Harmony) by Emperor Guangxu in 1888.

The palace was destroyed and rebuilt several times throughout its history, and the current structures date mostly from the late 19th and early 20th centuries.The palace is known for its beautiful gardens, lakes, and architectural structures, which were designed to reflect the natural beauty of the surrounding area.

The palace's main feature is Longevity Hill, which is covered in temples and pavilions, including the Hall of Benevolence and Longevity, the Hall of Jade Ripples, and the Tower of Buddhist Incense.The palace also features the Kunming Lake, which is the largest man-made lake in China. Visitors can take a boat ride on the lake to see the various temples and pavilions from the water.

The palace also has a number of bridges, including the Seventeen-Arch Bridge, which is the longest of its kind in China.In addition to its architectural and landscaping features, the Summer Palace is also known for its collection of artwork and artifacts. The palace houses a number of statues, paintings, and calligraphy works, many of which were created by famous Chinese artists of the past.

The Summer Palace was declared a UNESCO World Heritage Site in 1998, and is considered one of the most important cultural sites in China. It is a popular tourist destination and receives millions of visitors each year.

The Summer Palace is a magnificent architectural and landscaping masterpiece, with a rich cultural and historical significance. It reflects the luxurious lifestyle of the emperors of the past and showcases the art and craftsmanship of ancient China. The palace continues to be a source of inspiration and wonder for visitors from all over the world.

In addition to its architectural and landscaping features, the Summer Palace also has a number of important historical and cultural sites within its grounds. The palace was not only used as a recreational retreat for the imperial family, but also as a place for them to conduct government affairs and receive dignitaries.

One of the most notable structures within the palace is the Hall of Benevolence and Longevity, which was the main residence of the empress dowager Cixi. Cixi, who was one of the most powerful women in Chinese history, used the palace as a base of operations for her government and spent a significant portion of her later years there. The Hall of Benevolence and Longevity is now open to the public and contains many of Cixi's personal artifacts, including her throne and a collection of her calligraphy works.

Another important site within the palace is the Long Corridor, which is a covered walkway that runs along the shore of Kunming Lake.

The corridor is over 700 meters long and is adorned with over 14,000 colorful paintings, depicting scenes from Chinese folklore, history and legends. This corridor is considered one of the most important cultural and historical sites in China.

The palace also contains a number of temples and shrines, including the Temple of Buddhist Virtue, which is the largest Buddhist temple in the palace. The temple houses a number of statues and artifacts related to Buddhism and is a popular place for visitors to make offerings and pray for good luck.

The Summer Palace also has a number of museums within its grounds, including the Bronze Gallery, which houses a collection of ancient bronze artifacts and sculptures, and the Garden Museum, which showcases the history and development of the palace's gardens and landscaping.

In conclusion, the Summer Palace is not only a beautiful architectural and landscaping masterpiece, but also an important cultural and historical site. It provides visitors with a glimpse into the lives of the imperial family and the history of China, and showcases the art and craftsmanship of the past.

The palace continues to be a source of inspiration and wonder for visitors from all over the world, and is a must-see destination for anyone interested in Chinese culture and history.

Chapter Ten

Mode Of Transportation In China

China has a diverse and extensive transportation system that includes various modes such as rail, road, water, and air. The most widely used modes of transportation in China are trains and buses. The country has the world's largest high-speed rail network, which makes it easy to travel between major cities.

Buses are also a popular and affordable option for shorter distances. Additionally, China also has a growing network of urban and inter-city subway systems, as well as many airports and ports for air and water travel. Personal cars and bicycles are also widely used in urban areas.

In addition to the modes of transportation I mentioned earlier, China also has a growing network of expressways and highways, making road travel more convenient and efficient. Taxis and ride-sharing services like Didi Chuxing are also widely available in cities.

China's urban areas are also increasingly promoting the use of non-motorized transportation such as bicycles and e-bikes. Some cities have implemented bike-sharing programs to make it more convenient for people to use bicycles as a mode of transportation.

China's water transportation system is also well-developed, with many major rivers, lakes, and coastal areas having regular ferry services. Additionally, the country has a number of major ports that handle international trade and cargo.

Overall, China's transportation system is constantly evolving and expanding to meet the needs of its rapidly growing population and economy.

Chapter Eleven

Accommodation In China

China is a vast country with a diverse range of accommodation options available. From luxury hotels to budget hostels, there is something for everyone.

Luxury Hotels: China is home to some of the world's most luxurious hotels, such as the Ritz-Carlton, Four Seasons, and Mandarin Oriental. These hotels offer high-end amenities such as spas, gyms, and fine dining restaurants. They are typically located in major cities such as Beijing, Shanghai, and Hong Kong. Prices for these hotels can be quite high, with rooms starting at around $300 per night.

Business Hotels: For those traveling on business, there are many mid-range hotels that offer comfortable accommodation and modern facilities. These hotels are often located near business districts and have meeting rooms and business centers. They usually have restaurants and bars on site, and prices for rooms start at around $100 per night.

Budget Hotels: For those traveling on a budget, there are many budget hotels and hostels available in China. These can be found in major cities and tourist destinations. Prices for rooms start at around $20 per night. Some budget hotels may not have as many amenities as luxury or business hotels, but they offer clean, comfortable accommodation.

Apartments: Another option for accommodation in China is to rent an apartment. This can be a good choice for those planning to stay for a longer period or for families. There are many websites and apps, such as Airbnb and booking . Com, where you can find apartments for rent. Prices vary depending on the location and size of the apartment, but they are generally more affordable than hotels.

Homestays: Another great way to experience Chinese culture is to stay with a local family. Homestays are becoming increasingly popular in China, and they offer a unique and authentic way to experience local life. Many homestays offer meals and activities as part of the package, and prices are usually quite affordable.

Another popular accommodation option in China ***is traditional Chinese inns or "Lao zhaos".*** These are typically found in more rural or scenic areas and offer a more authentic Chinese experience. They are often located near historical sites, temples, and other cultural attractions. They usually have simple, traditional Chinese-style rooms and may have shared bathrooms. Prices for these types of accommodations are usually quite affordable, starting at around $20 per night.

Another unique accommodation option in China is the ***capsule hotel.*** These are popular in urban areas and are designed for budget-conscious travelers. They typically feature small, capsule-like rooms with just enough space for a bed and a few basic amenities. They are often located near transportation hubs, making them a convenient choice for travelers on the go. Prices for capsule hotels start at around $20 per night.

For a more luxurious and unique stay, some travelers opt for a traditional Chinese courtyard house, also known as “Siheyuan”. These houses are typically found in historic areas such as the Hutongs in Beijing and have been converted into boutique hotels. They offer a glimpse into traditional Chinese architecture and lifestyle and provide a more intimate and authentic experience.

Prices for these types of accommodations can be quite high, starting at around $200 per night.

It's also important to note that there are many travel agencies and online booking platforms that offer special deals and discounts for accommodation in China. It's a good idea to do some research and compare prices before booking your stay.

Additionally, many hotels and hostels offer discounts for longer stays, so it may be more cost-effective to book a longer stay rather than multiple shorter stays.

In summary, accommodation in China is diverse and offers something for every traveler, whether you're looking for luxury, budget-friendly options, or traditional Chinese experiences.

It's important to research and plan ahead to find the best option for your needs and budget. From luxury hotels to budget hostels, traditional inns, courtyard houses, apartments, and homestays, the options are endless.

Chapter Twelve

What To Wear In China

China is a country with a rich culture and history, and its customs and traditions extend to the way people dress. As a visitor to China, it's important to be mindful of the country's customs and dress appropriately.

When it comes to traditional Chinese clothing, the most well-known is the cheongsam, a form-fitting, one-piece dress for women, and the Mao suit, a type of tunic suit for men.

These traditional garments are typically worn during special occasions such as weddings and festivals.

However, you are unlikely to see locals wearing these traditional garments in their daily lives.

In general, casual clothing is appropriate for most occasions in China. T-shirts and jeans are common, as are shorts and sandals in the summer. However, it's important to note that showing too much skin is considered impolite in China, so it's best to avoid revealing clothing. Additionally, it's best to avoid clothing with offensive or politically sensitive slogans or images.

When it comes to business attire, a suit and tie or a formal dress is appropriate for men and women. It's also considered polite to dress more formally when visiting places of worship or government buildings.

In terms of footwear, it's best to wear comfortable shoes that are easy to walk in as you will be doing a lot of walking. Avoid wearing open-toe shoes or sandals as they are considered informal.

Overall, it's important to dress modestly and respectfully when visiting China. Avoid clothing with offensive or politically sensitive slogans or images, and dress conservatively, especially when visiting places of worship or government buildings.

It is also good to pack a light sweater or jacket, as the temperature can vary greatly between indoor and outdoor spaces.

It's also worth noting that China has a wide range of climates, from humid subtropical to subarctic, so it's important to check the weather forecast and pack accordingly. It's also a good idea to bring an umbrella or raincoat, as rain is common in many parts of the country.

In addition to the general guidelines for dressing in China, there are also some specific considerations to keep in mind depending on the region you will be visiting. In more rural or traditional areas, it's important to dress modestly and cover your legs and shoulders. Wearing shorts or revealing clothing can be considered disrespectful.

In these areas, it's also common for locals to dress in traditional clothing such as the cheongsam for women and the Mao suit for men.

In larger cities like Beijing and Shanghai, you'll see a wider range of styles and you'll have more flexibility when it comes to your clothing choices. However, it's still important to dress modestly and avoid revealing clothing.

When visiting historical or cultural sites, it's best to dress modestly and cover your legs and shoulders. Many sites will have dress codes, and you may be denied entry if you're not dressed appropriately.

It's also important to consider the season when packing for your trip to China. The weather can vary greatly depending on the region and time of year. In the summer, it can be very hot and humid, so lightweight, breathable clothing is best. In the winter, it can be very cold, so warm clothing and a coat are necessary.

In terms of accessories, it's important to keep in mind that China is a conservative country and it's best to avoid wearing anything too flashy or revealing. Jewelry should be kept to a minimum, and tattoos should be covered if possible.

In general, the key to dressing in China is to dress modestly, respectfully, and comfortably. Avoiding revealing clothing, and dressing conservatively when visiting places of worship or government buildings. Pack for the weather forecast and be mindful of regional customs and traditions.

It's also a good idea to bring a few versatile, mix-and-match pieces that can be dressed up or down depending on the occasion. This will allow you to be prepared for any situation and ensure that you're dressed appropriately.

Overall, China is a great place to visit and the people are very friendly and welcoming. By following these guidelines and being mindful of local customs and traditions, you will be able to fully enjoy your trip and make the most of your time in China.

Chapter Thirteen

Foods And Drinks You Will Find In China

China is a vast country with a rich and diverse culinary tradition that spans thousands of years. The country's cuisine is known for its use of a wide variety of ingredients and cooking techniques, as well as its emphasis on balance, flavor, and nutrition.

One of the most popular foods in China is rice. It is the staple food for many Chinese people and is often served with meat or vegetable dishes.

Some popular rice dishes include fried rice, jasmine rice, and sticky rice.

Noodles are also a popular food in China, and can be found in a wide variety of dishes. Some popular noodle dishes include lo mein, chow mein, and hand-pulled noodles.

In Northern China, wheat-based foods such as steamed buns, dumplings, and pancakes are popular. These foods are often filled with meat, vegetables or a combination of both.

Seafood is also a staple in Chinese cuisine, particularly in coastal regions. Some popular seafood dishes include steamed fish, shrimp, and crab.

Meat dishes are also popular in China, with pork, beef, and chicken being the most commonly used meats. Some popular meat dishes include Peking duck, Kung Pao chicken and sweet and sour pork.

Vegetable dishes are also an important part of Chinese cuisine. Some popular vegetable dishes include stir-fried vegetables, steamed vegetables, and hot and sour soup.

Chinese cuisine also includes a variety of soups and stews, such as wonton soup, hot and sour soup, and egg drop soup.

In terms of drinks, tea is the most popular beverage in China. Green tea, black tea, and oolong tea are all popular choices.

Herbal teas are also common, and are used for both their taste and their medicinal properties.

Alcoholic drinks are also popular in China, with rice wine and beer being the most commonly consumed. Baijiu is a strong liquor that is also popular in China.

China's culinary tradition is vast and diverse, with a wide variety of foods and drinks to discover and enjoy. From traditional regional cuisines to modern fusion dishes, Chinese cuisine offers something for everyone.

It's worth mentioning that China has a great deal of regional cuisines, for example Sichuan Cuisine is famous for its spicy and pungent flavors, Cantonese Cuisine is famous for its delicate and light flavors, and so on. Also, due to the large population and the long history of China, there are many other ethnic minority cuisines that have their unique characteristics.

Another important aspect of Chinese cuisine is the use of sauces and seasonings. Soy sauce, oyster sauce, hoisin sauce, and black bean sauce are all commonly used to add flavor to dishes. Other popular seasonings include ginger, garlic, and chili peppers. These ingredients are often used in combination to create complex and nuanced flavors.

Dim sum is a type of Cantonese cuisine that is popular in southern China, particularly in Hong Kong and Guangzhou. Dim sum is a style of dining that involves small, bite-sized dishes that are typically served in steamer baskets. These dishes can include dumplings, buns, and other small dishes.

Street food is also a popular aspect of Chinese cuisine, with a wide variety of snacks and meals available from street vendors. Some popular street foods include steamed buns, fried dumplings, and skewers of meat and vegetables.

Chinese cuisine also includes a wide variety of desserts and sweet treats. Some popular desserts include mooncakes, glutinous rice balls, and sweet soups made with fruits and grains.

It's also worth mentioning that Chinese cuisine has been heavily influenced by other cultures over the centuries. For example, Chinese cuisine has been heavily influenced by the culinary traditions of its neighboring countries, such as Japan, Korea, and Vietnam.

Additionally, the country has a long history of trade with other countries, which has led to the introduction of new ingredients and cooking techniques.

Overall, Chinese cuisine is a rich and diverse culinary tradition that offers something for everyone. With a wide variety of foods, drinks, and cooking styles, Chinese cuisine is a true reflection of the country's history and culture.

Whether you're a foodie or simply looking to try something new, Chinese cuisine is sure to delight and surprise you.

Chapter Fourteen

Things To Do When You Spend Time In China

China is a vast and culturally rich country with a history that stretches back thousands of years. Whether you're a first-time visitor or a seasoned traveler, there are plenty of things to see and do when you spend time in China. Here are just a few suggestions for how to make the most of your trip:

1.Visit the Great Wall of China: This iconic structure is one of the most famous landmarks in the world, and it's a must-see destination when you're in China.

There are several sections of the wall that are open to visitors, and each one offers a unique experience. The most popular sections are Badaling, Mutianyu, and Jinshanling.

2.Explore the Forbidden City: The Forbidden City is a palace complex in Beijing that was the home of the Chinese emperors for over 500 years. It's a UNESCO World Heritage site, and it's one of the best examples of traditional Chinese architecture.

Visitors can explore the palace's many courtyards, halls, and pavilions, and learn about the history of the Chinese imperial court.

3.See the Terracotta Warriors: The Terracotta Warriors are a group of life-size statues that were discovered in the 1970s in Xi'an. They were buried with the first emperor of China, and they are considered one of the greatest archaeological finds of the 20th century. Visitors can see the warriors up close in the museum built around the site.

4.Visit the Shanghai Tower: The Shanghai Tower is the second tallest building in the world and offers incredible views of the city. Visitors can take an elevator to the observation deck and see the city from a bird's eye view.

5.Explore the Pandas in Chengdu: Chengdu is the home of the Giant Pandas and you can explore the Panda Breeding and Research Base where you can see the pandas up close.

6.Visit the Leshan Giant Buddha: The Leshan Giant Buddha is a 71-meter tall statue of Maitreya Buddha carved into a cliff in Sichuan province. It's the largest stone Buddha statue in the world and is a UNESCO World Heritage Site.

7.Take a cruise on the Li River: The Li River is one of the most picturesque rivers in China, with its towering limestone cliffs and picturesque villages. Taking a cruise on the river is a great way to see the scenery and learn about the local culture.

8.Visit the Yellow Mountains: The Yellow Mountains are a range of mountains in Anhui province that are known for their natural beauty. Visitors can hike the trails, take cable cars to the summit, or take in the views from a hot air balloon.

9.Visit a Traditional Chinese Garden: China is known for its traditional gardens, which are designed to be a reflection of nature. Some of the most famous gardens include the Summer Palace and the Garden of the Master of the Nets in Suzhou.

10.Try the local cuisine: Chinese food is famous around the world, and there are many different regional cuisines to try.

Some popular dishes include Peking duck, hotpot, and dumplings. Be sure to also try some street food while you're in China.

These are just a few suggestions for things to see and do when you spend time in China. With so much to see and do, you'll need to plan your trip carefully to make the most of your time.

Remember to also take the time to explore the local culture and meet the local people. China is a fascinating country with a rich history and culture, and it's well worth a visit.

Chapter Fifteen

Health And Safety Tips

When traveling to China, there are several health and safety considerations to keep in mind in order to have a safe and enjoyable trip.

1.Health concerns: Before traveling to China, it is important to be up to date on all routine vaccinations, as well as any additional vaccinations that may be recommended for the area you will be visiting. It is also a good idea to bring a basic first aid kit, including items such as pain relievers, bandages, and any prescription medications you may need.

2.Air pollution: Some cities in China have high levels of air pollution, which can be harmful to your health. It is a good idea to check the air quality in the areas you will be visiting before your trip and to take precautions such as wearing a mask or staying indoors during times of high pollution.

3.Food safety: When eating in China, be sure to choose food from reputable sources and avoid street vendors. Also, be sure to wash your hands frequently and avoid consuming raw or undercooked food, which can increase your risk of food poisoning.

4.Water safety: Tap water in China is not considered safe to drink, so it is a good idea to stick to bottled water and be sure to check the seal before drinking.

5.Transportation safety: When traveling by car or bus in China, be aware that traffic can be chaotic and roads can be poorly maintained. It is important to wear seat belts and be aware of your surroundings at all times.

6.Scams: Be aware of common scams in China, such as fake taxi drivers, street vendors selling counterfeit goods, and unlicensed tour guides.

7.Travel insurance: Make sure you have comprehensive travel insurance before traveling to China, in case of any unexpected health or safety issues.

8.Emergency contact: Have emergency contact information with you, including the number for the nearest embassy or consulate, in case of an emergency.

By keeping these health and safety tips in mind, you can help ensure that your trip to China is a safe and enjoyable one.

www.ingramcontent.com/pod-product-compliance
Lightning Source LLC
LaVergne TN
LVHW080554160826
845677LV00010B/1848